RADIANTLY QUEER:

AFFIRMING OUR AUTHENTIC LIVES

ALSO BY LIAM SAWYER

Wishes Of Love
Whispers Of Hope

RADIANTLY QUEER:

AFFIRMING OUR AUTHENTIC LIVES

LIAM SAWYER

Published in the United States by Liam Sawyer
an imprint of Sawyer Original
New York, NY

Author: Liam Sawyer

First Edition: May 15, 2024

ISBN: 979-8-9890576-0-3 (Paperback)
ISBN: 979-8-9890576-4-1(ePub Edition)

1. Self-Improvement--Non-Fiction. 2. LGBTQ+ Themes--Poetry.
3. Affirmations--Inspirational & Personal Growth. 4. Queer Voices--LGBTQ+ Literature.

Library of Congress Control Number: 2023916439

For permissions or any questions, please contact:
Liam Sawyer
Website: liamsawyer.com

Disclaimer: This book is intended to provide helpful and informative material on the
subjects addressed. It is sold with the understanding that the author and publisher are
not engaged in rendering professional services in the book. If the reader requires personal assistance or advice, a competent professional should be consulted. The author and
publisher specifically disclaim any responsibility for any liability, loss, or risk, personal
or otherwise, which is incurred as a consequence, directly or indirectly, of the use and
application of any of the contents of this book.

For those who are still finding their way out of the closet.

Your journey is your own and your courage does not go unnoticed. No matter where you are in your journey, know that you are not alone and that you are deserving of love and acceptance just as you are. May this book serve as a beacon of hope, affirmation, and strength for you.

TABLE OF CONTENTS

Prelude

Welcome

In the quiet corners of our hearts, in the hushed whispers barely escaping our lips, lie stories untold, identities unexpressed, and love unshared. This book is a tribute to those stories, those identities, and that love.

In a world that often demands us to fit neatly into boxes, it can be a daunting task to embrace who we truly are, especially when we don't align with societal norms. The journey of self-discovery is one filled with fear, confusion, courage, and ultimately, liberation.

This book is a testament to the struggle and beauty inherent in this journey. It's a celebration of authenticity, resilience, and the power of living one's truth. It's a call to acknowledge and affirm those who are still navigating their path, still negotiating their terms of existence, still gathering the courage to step out of the closet.

As you turn these pages, may you find echoes of your own experiences, validation of your feelings, and the comfort of knowing you're not alone. May this book inspire you to embrace your true self, to live fearlessly, and to love openly.

Welcome to a journey of self-love, acceptance, and the freedom to be who you truly are.

02
Introduction

The Journey of This Book

Each book has its genesis, a spark that ignites a flame of creation. This one began as whispers of personal experiences, hushed conversations with friends, and the ever-present undercurrents of a community yearning for representation, understanding, and solace.

My life, like many others, has been a tapestry of joys, challenges, love, and learning. From the corridors of my high school, filled with anticipatory whispers and then triumphant shouts of coming out, to the bustling streets of New York that embraced a young boy from Ukraine, every moment left an indelible mark. Each experience whispered a tale of authenticity, acceptance, and resilience.

The inspiration for Radiantly Queer stemmed from two places: a personal longing for a guide during my own moments of doubt and the stories of countless others in our community, each one echoing the need for a beacon amidst the fog. Over time, it became apparent that while the LGBTQ+ community is vast and diverse, many of us journey through similar landscapes of emotion, self-discovery, and identity.

The purpose of this book is simple yet profound: to offer a safe haven for reflection, validation, and empowerment. I felt an immense need for a resource that wasn't just about defining our identities but celebrating them, a tool that nurtured both the soul and the self.

Our community thrives on the stories we share, the connections we make, and the love we spread. This book is a testament to that spirit, and I hope it serves as a companion on your journey, a reminder that your story, no matter how it unfolds, is a vital chapter in the grand narrative of life.

With every page, may you find pieces of yourself, and in every word, the validation that you, as you are, matter.

The Journey of This Book

Why Affirmations?

Words, simple as they may seem, are instruments of immense power. They shape our realities, sculpt our beliefs, and carve pathways in our minds. In the realm of personal growth, affirmations serve as the chisel with which we can craft our desired realities.

At their core, affirmations are positive declarations, intentional phrases meant to counteract and challenge the internalized negativities we often unknowingly harbor. These negativities could be remnants of past traumas, societal pressures, or self-doubt that's accumulated over time. Affirmations rise as defiant answers to these shadows, reminding us of our intrinsic worth, strength, and potential.

The act of repeating an affirmation, either verbally or mentally, creates a kind of cognitive resonance. Each repetition reinforces a neural pathway, slowly altering our ingrained beliefs and habits. It's akin to tracing over a pencil sketch with a pen, making the lines clearer, bolder, and more defined with each pass. Over time, the persistent positivity of these affirmations begins to overpower the doubts and negativities, embedding themselves deeply into our subconscious.

Beyond the science, affirmations are acts of self-love. In a world that often challenges our identities, especially within the LGBTQ+ community, affirmations become our personal anthems. They are daily reminders that we not only belong but are deserving of love, respect, and all the beauty life has to offer.

Through Radiantly Queer, my hope is for these affirmations to be your daily companions, your whispered strength in moments of doubt, and your shouted joy in times of triumph. May they guide you towards a profound belief in yourself, and in doing so, illuminate the path to living authentically.

Navigating the Landscape

As you venture into the pages of Radiantly Queer, consider this a roadmap, guiding you through the various terrains of exploration and introspection contained within. Each section has been meticulously crafted, not just to inform, but to inspire and instill a deeper under-standing of oneself and the broader LGBTQ+ community.

Affirmations

These are the heartbeats of this journey. Crafted as mantras of self-love, resilience, and acceptance, these phrases resonate with the energy to shift perspectives and bolster self-belief. They are words of power, meant to be whispered, shouted, felt, and internalized.

Journal Prompts

Delving into the inner recesses of the mind, these prompts are your invitation to introspect. They offer gateways to explore, dissect, and understand the myriad emotions, experiences, and aspirations that shape you.

Quotes

Glimpses into the wisdom of many who've walked this path, or parallel ones, before us. These pearls of wisdom, sometimes poignant, sometimes uplifting, always resonate with universal truths of the human experience.

Poetry Pages

Within these leaves lie spaces for your heart's utterances, your soul's whispers, and your mind's musings. Through verses and rhymes, give voice to your unspoken emotions, memories, and dreams. These pages stand as an invitation to the dance of words and feelings, capturing the essence of moments, fleeting or eternal.

Descriptive Pages for the LGBTQ+ Community

Knowledge is power. These pages dive deep into the diverse spectrum of LGBTQ+ identities, offering clarity, understanding, and validation. They are a testament to the vibrant mosaic of our community.

As you traverse through Radiantly Queer, remember that every individual's journey is unique. Whether you soar through each section, or tread with gentle caution, know that the journey is yours, and every step, every word, every reflection is a stride towards a deeper connection with your authentic self.

Let the exploration begin.

How to Use This Book

Radiantly Queer isn't just a book—it's a tool, a companion, and a sanctuary. While its pages provide structure and guidance, remember that this journey is inherently personal. Here are some suggestions on how to approach each section, but always trust your intuition and pace:

Affirmations

Start or end your day with one. Let its words seep into your morning routine or your nightly reflections. You might choose to focus on a single affirmation for several days, allowing its message to deeply resonate, or switch daily for varied inspiration. Keep them close. Write your favorite ones on sticky notes and place them around your living space—mirrors, fridges, or even your workspace. Let them serve as frequent reminders of your intrinsic worth and strength.

Journal Prompts

Dedicate a specific time each week to sit down with these. Perhaps it's a quiet Sunday morning or a reflective Friday night. The consistency can help create a ritual of introspection. Don't rush. If a prompt stirs deep emotions or memories, give yourself the time and space to explore those feelings. It's okay to revisit the same prompt multiple times, as our perspectives and insights evolve.

Quotes

Reflect on their wisdom. When a quote particularly strikes you, perhaps take a moment to journal about why it resonates. What personal experiences or feelings does it evoke?

Poetry Pages

Dive in at any moment. There's no prescribed path; instead, let your curiosity or current emotional state guide your reading journey. Whether daily, weekly, or during moments of quiet reflection, let these poems resonate with your soul. Seek connection, not judgment. As you traverse these pages, remember that each poem is an echo of a moment, a sentiment, a shared human experience. Allow yourself to be immersed, to question, to feel—knowing that in poetry, every emotion finds its mirror.

Descriptive Pages for the LGBTQ+ Community

Refer to them often. Whether you're seeking understanding, validation, or simply a reminder of the community's vast and beautiful spectrum, these pages are here to enlighten and empower.

Lastly, while this guide offers a structure, remember there's no right or wrong way to navigate Radiantly Queer. It's designed to adapt to your journey, not dictate it. Let your heart, mood, and needs guide your path through its pages, and embrace the exploration of your authentic self.

A Safe Space

In a world that often demands conformity, where differences can be met with misunderstanding, and where expressing one's true self can be a courageous act, this book stands as a sanctuary. As you turn these pages, know that every word was crafted with love, acceptance, and understanding.

Each section is an embrace. Each affirmation, a validation. Each journal prompt, an invitation to introspect and reconnect. Within these confines, there are no judgments. No demands. Just a gentle reminder that you are deserving of love, respect, and understanding.

While the outside world may sometimes be chaotic and unyielding, here, you are free. Free to explore. Free to question. Free to be vulnerable. Free to be you. This book is more than just pages bound together; it's a haven for your heart and soul.

So, as you journey through its depths, be as authentic, raw, and true as you wish. This is your safe space, a place where your spirit can breathe, where your truths can unfurl, and where every part of you is welcome.

Welcome to your refuge.

To The Reader

From one soul to another, I extend a heartfelt greeting as you embark on this journey. With every word inked on these pages, I hope you feel the resonance of a community that sees you, understands you, and stands with you.

Life, with its myriad of hues, can sometimes paint strokes of confusion, isolation, and doubt. Yet, it's equally capable of crafting moments of clarity, connection, and sheer joy. As you navigate the mosaic of your experiences, remember that every shade, every emotion, and every challenge contributes to the masterpiece that is you.

Your voice, even if hushed or roaring, possesses a timbre that is profoundly unique and irreplaceable. As you delve into this book, may you rediscover facets of yourself that have been waiting to shimmer, aspects that have been longing for acknowledgment, and parts that are eager to find their melody.

While this journey is uniquely yours, know that you are not walking it alone. Through shared experiences, collective wisdom, and the bonds of solidarity, a tapestry of love and understanding is interwoven in every corner of our community.

May this book serve as a mirror, reflecting your worth and potential back to you. May it be a beacon, illuminating paths of self-love, acceptance, and authenticity. But above all, may it remind you that your existence is a gift, not just to those who know and love you, but to a world that is brighter simply because you are in it.

With warmth and hope,
Liam Sawyer

Your journey to affirming your truth starts now.

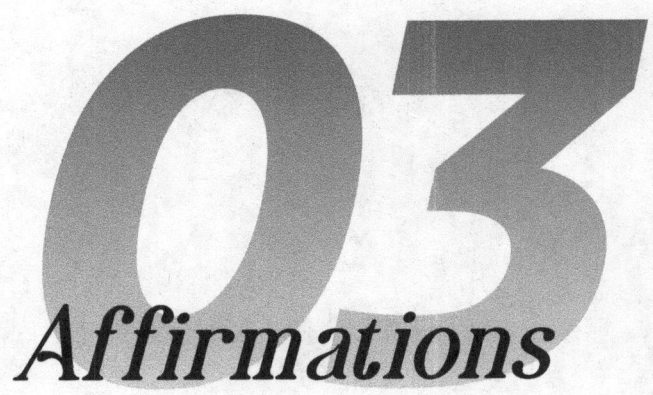

03
Affirmations

Self-Love & Identity

In the vast canvas of the universe, my existence is a unique masterpiece.

My identity, with its hues and shades, tells a story that only I can narrate. Every brushstroke of my experiences, desires, and dreams validates my irreplaceable presence in this world.

Embrace this affirmation as a testament to your individuality and significance in this ever-expanding universe. It's essential to recognize and remember that your identity, like a painter's most cherished work, is formed through layers of experiences, choices, and introspections. Each element that makes up who you are— your sexuality, your aspirations, your challenges, and triumphs—adds depth and texture to your personal narrative. When you resonate with this affirmation, you are not only celebrating your unique existence but also reaffirming that your story is worthy of being told, heard, and respected. Remember, no one else can paint your story. Hold your brush with pride, and let your colors shine brightly.

The symphony of my heart plays a melody that's uniquely mine.

Amidst the crescendos and quiet moments, I recognize the beauty of my true self. My self-worth isn't measured by applause or critiques, but by the authentic rhythm I bring to life.

Life's journey is often compared to music, filled with high notes of joy, low notes of challenges, and the silences of reflection. The tune your heart plays is deeply personal, crafted from years of experiences, emotions, and growth. Just as in a symphony, where every instrument plays a vital role, your individuality adds to the beautiful orchestra of existence. It's imperative to remember that external validation, while often flattering, is transient. The most enduring and genuine validation comes from within, from acknowledging and celebrating your unique rhythm. The authenticity you bring to the world, unfiltered and true, is the most significant measure of your worth.

My journey of self-discovery is a sacred pilgrimage.

With every step, I uncover layers of my soul, finding treasures of wisdom and strength. I embrace the entirety of who I am, knowing that my identity is the compass guiding me to my true north.

Each of us embarks on a personal voyage of self-discovery, a pilgrimage that is as spiritual as it is profound. This journey isn't about reaching a particular destination but about understanding the depths of our own being. As we traverse through life, we encounter various challenges and joys, each peeling back a layer of our soul, revealing insights we might have never known. These discoveries are the gems that enrich our path, teaching us resilience, love, and purpose. By embracing every facet of our identity, we find clarity and direction. This internal compass doesn't just point north; it points to our truest self, a beacon guiding us through life's vast landscape.

The mirror reflects more than just my image; it captures the universe within me.

Every facet of my identity is a testament to endless possibilities and boundless love. I am a living testament to courage, evolution, and the magic of being truly, unapologetically me.

Each time we gaze into a mirror, we're not just seeing a physical reflection, but a deep, profound universe of experiences, dreams, and emotions. Our identity is a tapestry woven from threads of memories, lessons, passions, and love. It's a manifestation of countless moments, decisions, and stories that culminate into the person we see. Celebrating oneself is not just about embracing the evident but acknowledging the hidden depths, the myriad possibilities that make us who we are. Your existence is a testament to the resilience of the human spirit, the beauty of evolution, and the pure magic that comes from being your most genuine self.

I am the guardian of my own galaxy, with stars shaped by dreams and nebulae born from passions.

My identity is not fixed but expands infinitely, embracing change, growth, and the luminous beauty of self-acceptance. I shine brightest when I allow myself to simply be.

The universe within each of us is vast, mysterious, and ever-expanding. Much like the galaxies that evolve, shift, and shine, our identities are in a constant state of flux, shaped by experiences, dreams, and intrinsic passions. Being the guardian of one's internal cosmos means understanding and appreciating its dynamic nature. Instead of resisting change, it's about flowing with it, letting each transformation enhance our luminance. True brilliance is achieved not when we fit into predefined molds, but when we bask in the liberating power of self-acceptance, allowing ourselves the freedom to exist without limitations.

Belonging & Acceptance

Within the vast tapestry of humanity, my thread weaves a story of resilience and beauty.

My place isn't determined by society's design but by the intricate patterns I form with others. I am intertwined with a community that sees me, values me, and embraces my every hue.

Each individual represents a unique and irreplaceable thread in the grand tapestry of existence. Your story, rich with trials and triumphs, is a testament to the indomitable spirit of perseverance and the allure of individuality. While society might have its notions and templates, true belonging arises from the intricate relationships and connections we nurture. Your value isn't just in standing out but also in how you intertwine with others, creating a shared narrative of understanding, acceptance, and collective strength. It's in these bonds with your community that you find affirmation, appreciation, and a genuine embrace of all that you are.

The world is an orchestra, and my voice adds a unique note to its song.

Even when I feel adrift in a sea of voices, I remember that I am sought after, cherished, and irreplaceable. In the chorus of existence, I find my harmony by simply being myself.

In the grand symphony of life, every individual has a unique tone and resonance. There might be moments of self-doubt, where you feel lost in the vastness of the chorus, but it's essential to remember that your voice has its unique timbre and essence. It's not about being the loudest or the most pronounced, but about the authenticity and heart you bring to the melody. You are an irreplaceable note, contributing to the collective harmony. By embracing your true self and giving voice to your passions, dreams, and beliefs, you not only find your place in the orchestra of life but also inspire others to find and cherish their unique notes.

The universe carved out a space for me long before I arrived.

It anticipated my laughter, tears, dreams, and the love I'd share. I belong, not because the world permits me, but because I etch my essence into every moment, claiming my rightful space.

Your existence is no accident. The universe, in its vastness and complexity, had a design for you, an understanding of the spectrum of emotions and experiences you'd traverse. Your significance isn't predicated on external validation or societal acceptance; it's intrinsic. The space you occupy in the world isn't just a physical one but an emotional, spiritual, and temporal one. Every emotion you feel, every dream you chase, and every bit of love you share leaves an indelible mark. The true essence of belonging stems from the deep realization that you're not merely passing through, but actively shaping, influencing, and etching your narrative in the annals of time.

In the dance of life, my steps — whether tentative or bold — find their rhythm.

Even when shadows of doubt loom, the glow of acceptance from within and from my community lights my way. Every turn, twirl, and pause is a testament to my unyielding right to belong.

Life, in its essence, is a dance. A dance of emotions, experiences, and expressions. Whether you're taking your first uncertain steps or confidently gliding through, your unique rhythm and style have a purpose. Doubts, much like shadows, may momentarily obscure your path, but the inner radiance of self-belief combined with the support and acceptance from your community can dispel them. Every movement you make—be it an adventurous twirl, a contemplative pause, or an assertive leap—affirms your innate right to exist, to express, and to belong. Embrace your dance, for it is an ode to your resilience, individuality, and the love that surrounds you.

My heart, with its boundless capacity for love, recognizes its tribe.

In the silent nods of understanding, the embrace of acceptance, and the resonance of shared experiences, I am reminded that I am not alone. My journey, though unique, intertwines with countless others, forging bonds of unspoken kinship.

Our hearts, vast and deep, possess an intuitive ability to identify connections that resonate on a profound level. This isn't always about shared histories or common backgrounds but rather an intangible understanding, a shared frequency of emotion and experience. Life, in its vast tapestry, brings moments of solitude, but these moments are punctuated with profound connections — those silent affirmations, warm embraces, and moments of shared laughter or tears. Every step you take on your distinct path is accompanied, in parallel, by others on their journeys. These journeys, though individually charted, often converge, intertwining in moments of empathy and shared understanding, reinforcing the universal truth of interconnectedness.

Overcoming Internal & External Challenges

When storms of doubt and judgment rage around and within me, I stand firm in the knowledge of my worth.

These challenges, no matter how formidable, are but fleeting clouds. With resilience and grace, I navigate through them, emerging stronger, with a clearer vision of my authentic self.

Throughout the journey of life, challenges, doubts, and judgments often appear as tumultuous storms, threatening to obscure our path and diminish our light. But these tempests, regardless of their intensity, are temporary. It's essential to anchor oneself in the enduring knowledge of personal worth and value. Every storm you face and every shadow you navigate through acts as a refining process. These experiences, instead of diminishing you, chisel away uncertainties, revealing a stronger, more defined version of yourself. With each trial, you're not just surviving but evolving, gaining clarity, and inching closer to the most genuine version of who you are.

The opinions and biases of the world cannot cage the boundless spirit within me.

While I may encounter walls of misunderstanding and prejudice, I possess the strength to either climb over or break them down. My journey is proof of my enduring spirit and unyielding courage.

The world can be a cacophony of opinions, judgments, and biases. These external voices, often rooted in misunderstanding and prejudice, can sometimes seem insurmountable, like towering walls trying to enclose and define us. However, it's crucial to remember that our spirit is inherently limitless, unconfined by these walls. Your journey, marked by encounters with such barriers, is a testament to your resilience. It showcases that with determination and courage, walls can be transcended or dismantled. You aren't defined by the limitations others set for you but by the boundless vigor of your spirit and the courage you demonstrate in staying true to yourself.

Every internal battle I face is a step toward deeper self-awareness and growth.

My struggles are not signs of weakness but markers of my evolution. As I confront and conquer them, I forge a path that illuminates hope for both myself and those who walk beside me.

Life is a series of challenges, each presenting an opportunity to delve deeper into oneself. These internal battles, whether they arise from doubt, fear, or external pressures, are transformative experiences. They aren't indicators of deficiencies or frailties; instead, they highlight the ongoing process of personal refinement and discovery. As you grapple with these struggles, you aren't just moving past them but also drawing invaluable lessons and strengths. Moreover, the journey you embark on is not solitary. Every hurdle you overcome, every insight you gain, serves as a beacon for others, offering reassurance and inspiring hope.

The weight of societal expectations cannot drown the voice that sings my truth.

When external noise threatens to overshadow, I tune into the melody of my heart — a song of defiance, love, and unwavering authenticity. I am the composer of my life's symphony, and its notes are mine to define.

Living authentically, especially amidst a world brimming with external pressures and societal mandates, requires courage. Often, the collective voice of society can be loud, attempting to dictate, influence, or sway our personal narratives. But deep within, there lies an intrinsic voice, a unique melody that resonates with our truth. This melody, enriched with individual experiences, emotions, and dreams, serves as a grounding force. Whenever the cacophony of societal expectations becomes overwhelming, remember to center yourself by listening to your heart's song. By doing so, you affirm your agency, autonomy, and the undeniable right to design your life on your terms.

Challenges, both internal and external, are but tests of my character and resolve.

With every hardship, I gather stories of perseverance, lessons in empathy, and a deeper understanding of my purpose. I am not defined by the battles I face, but by the grace and tenacity with which I overcome them.

Life is an intricate tapestry of experiences — some joyous, some challenging. Every challenge, whether it manifests internally as personal doubts or externally as obstacles, offers a unique opportunity for growth. Facing these challenges head-on, with grit and grace, adds chapters of resilience, understanding, and insight to your life's story. These experiences don't serve to detract from your essence but enrich it, providing depth, perspective, and wisdom. It's vital to internalize that it's not the presence of challenges that shapes you but the manner in which you navigate and surmount them. Your journey, with its highs and lows, is a testament to the enduring spirit within.

Healing & Growth

In the tender moments of healing, I rediscover the depths of my strength.

Wounds of the past, though they may leave scars, are also the gateways to profound growth. As I tend to each one, I sow seeds of wisdom, resilience, and an ever-expanding love for myself.

Healing is a powerful and transformative journey. It requires vulnerability, introspection, and immense courage. Every wound, physical or emotional, carries with it a lesson, an insight that often reveals hidden reservoirs of strength and resilience. By actively engaging in the process of healing, by acknowledging and nurturing these wounds, you are not only mending but also growing. These scars, rather than serving as mere reminders of pain, become symbols of battles won, of wisdom gained, and of a renewed commitment to self-love. Remember, every step taken towards healing is also a step towards a more empowered, enlightened self.

The tapestry of my life, with its light and shadows, is a testament to transformation.

Each challenge I've faced, every tear I've shed, fuels my journey towards a brighter, more authentic self. My past does not bind me; instead, it propels my evolution.

Life is a dynamic, ever-evolving journey characterized by myriad experiences, both joyous and challenging. This journey, with its peaks and valleys, paints a vibrant tapestry of transformation. Every obstacle overcome, every moment of vulnerability, adds depth and dimension to your narrative. These experiences, rather than acting as chains of the past, serve as catalysts, spurring growth and evolution. Embracing both the light and shadows of your story is crucial, for it's in this holistic acceptance that you find liberation. Your past, with its myriad hues, doesn't tether you; it provides momentum, guiding you towards an even more authentic, luminous future.

With every breath, I embrace the rhythms of healing and growth.

The universe, in its boundless compassion, supports my journey towards wholeness. I trust the process, knowing that each step, no matter how small, brings me closer to the person I am destined to become.

Life is an intricate dance of experiences, emotions, and evolution. With each breath, we engage with the world, drawing from its energy and imbuing it with our essence. Trusting in this process is essential, especially when we find ourselves on paths of healing and self-discovery. The universe, with its infinite wisdom and benevolence, orchestrates a supportive backdrop, guiding and nurturing us as we journey towards our most authentic selves. Embracing the journey, in all its unpredictability and beauty, allows us to truly understand and value our evolution. Every moment, every experience, regardless of its magnitude, contributes to the tapestry of who we are and who we are becoming.

Growth is the beautiful dance of letting go and embracing anew.

As I release the burdens and narratives that no longer serve me, I create space for joy, love, and experiences that align with my true essence. The cycles of healing are not only about mending but also about blooming in unexpected ways.

The essence of growth lies in its duality – it's a delicate balance between holding on and letting go. In the dance of life, we gather stories, experiences, and narratives. But as time unfolds, we often find that some of these no longer resonate with our evolving selves. Letting go of such burdens or outdated narratives paves the way for rejuvenation and discovery. It creates a sanctuary where joy, love, and experiences that reflect our true essence can flourish. Healing, in this context, becomes a transformative force, not just about patching up wounds but also about rediscovering and redefining oneself. Embracing these cycles of healing and growth allows us to flourish and bloom in ways we might never have imagined.

In the sanctuary of my soul, I nurture the promise of renewal.

Every experience, even those steeped in pain, provides fertile ground for growth. I cherish the lessons, honor my progress, and move forward with the unwavering belief that the best of me is still unfolding.

The soul is a profound space of introspection, reflection, and immense potential. Within its depths, we find the capacity for continuous renewal and rejuvenation. Life, with its myriad experiences, serves as a teacher, offering lessons in both joy and pain. While it's natural to wish away the painful moments, it's essential to recognize that these experiences often carry the most potent seeds of growth.

Embracing every lesson, be it bitter or sweet, allows for a richer, deeper understanding of oneself and the world. Celebrating the journey, acknowledging every milestone, however minor, reinforces self-belief and optimism. Remember, life is not a static entity; it's a dynamic continuum.

Resilience & Hope

The storms I've weathered are not simply tales of survival but epics of my resilience.

Each tempest has fortified my spirit, teaching me that even in the darkest moments, the flame of hope remains undiminished. I carry forward not just memories, but a legacy of unyielding strength.

Life's storms, both literal and metaphorical, are profound experiences that shape our narrative. They aren't merely episodes of endurance but are emblematic of the inner fortitude we possess. Every challenge, every tempest faced, does more than just test our mettle; it refines and reinforces it. Within these storms, there's an inherent lesson of hope and persistence — even when surrounded by overwhelming darkness, the innate light of hope continues to shine brightly, guiding us forward. As you reflect upon these experiences, understand that they are not just fleeting memories but pillars of strength, contributing to a legacy of resilience. This legacy isn't just a testament to your past, but a beacon for your future.

In the mosaic of my life, every crack and fracture only adds to my intricate beauty.

The challenges I've faced, and the resilience I've shown, interweave to create a testament to the human spirit's indomitable hope. My journey is a vibrant testament to perseverance in the face of adversity.

Life, much like a mosaic, is a compilation of experiences, moments, and choices. Each piece, regardless of its perceived imperfection, contributes to the larger picture. Just as cracks in a mosaic render it unique, the challenges and setbacks we face in life add depth, character, and authenticity to our narrative. These imperfections aren't flaws but rather validations of our resilience and ability to persevere.

Every hurdle, every crack, stands as a testament to the human spirit's unwavering determination and hope. Embracing this perspective allows us to view our journey not as a series of fragmented events but as a cohesive, vibrant testament to the beauty of overcoming adversity and forging ahead, even when the path seems uncertain.

With every setback, I plant seeds of hope that bloom into gardens of resilience.

Though moments of despair may visit, they are fleeting guests in the grand tapestry of my life. Hope is my eternal companion, guiding me through the unknown and illuminating my path with possibilities.

Life is a dynamic interplay of highs and lows. Setbacks, while challenging, are also opportunities for growth and reinvention. Rather than perceiving them as insurmountable obstacles, envision them as the fertile soil where seeds of hope are sown. With nurturing and patience, these seeds blossom into vibrant gardens of resilience, overshadowing transient moments of despair. Hope is not just a fleeting emotion but a steadfast guide. It casts its luminous light even in the darkest corners, revealing pathways and potentials previously unseen. Embracing hope is to acknowledge the cyclical nature of life, where every ending is also a beginning, and every challenge, a gateway to newfound strength.

The resilience I've cultivated is not just a shield against the world but a beacon for others.

My journey, strewn with obstacles and triumphs, lights the way for those seeking hope amidst despair. In my story, they find the assurance that they too can overcome, adapt, and flourish.

Resilience, cultivated through experiences and challenges, is a powerful testament to the human spirit. It not only serves as a protective armor for oneself but also shines as a guiding light for others navigating their storms. Sharing our journey, with its myriad of hurdles and victories, offers solace and inspiration to those feeling ensnared in despair. It whispers the empowering message that challenges can be surmounted, that transformation is possible, and that growth often sprouts from the most unexpected places. In the chronicles of our resilience, others find a mirror to their potential, realizing that they too possess the innate power to adapt, overcome, and thrive.

Hope is my north star, unwavering and luminous, guiding me through life's tumultuous seas.

No matter the challenges I face, the beacon of hope never dims. It reminds me of my inherent resilience, my capacity to dream, and the boundless potential that tomorrow holds.

Hope is not just an emotion; it is a compass that navigates us through the unpredictable waters of life. Like the unwavering north star in a vast night sky, hope serves as a constant, providing direction when our paths seem murky or insurmountable. Life will, inevitably, present us with challenges — some minor ripples, others turbulent storms. Yet, the brilliance of hope never wanes. It stands as a testament to our inner strength, our ability to envision brighter days, and the innate belief in the promise of tomorrow. Clinging to hope allows us to tap into our reservoir of resilience and to always remember that, regardless of today's circumstances, the horizon of tomorrow is replete with limitless possibilities.

Affirming Your Truth

In the sacred narrative of my life, every word, pause, and exclamation is penned by the authentic rhythm of my heart.

I honor the truth that pulses within me, embracing its wisdom, its nuances, and its unyielding call. My truth is my compass, guiding me to the shores of genuine existence.

Our personal narrative is a powerful testament to our unique experiences, thoughts, and feelings. Like a book that only we can author, every chapter, every sentence of our life holds profound meaning. It's important to understand that our heart, with its innate wisdom and authenticity, is the true scribe of this story. By honoring this inner truth, we embrace a more genuine and fulfilling existence. This truth is not merely a concept but a guiding force, leading us towards a life of purpose and alignment with our deepest self.

I wear my truth as a cloak woven from threads of experience, introspection, and revelation.

It guards me from the cold winds of conformity and the rains of doubt. By draping myself in its warmth, I stand tall, resolute, and undeniably me.

Truth, both profound and deeply personal, becomes a protective armor when we embrace and honor it. Like a meticulously woven cloak, our truth is constructed from the myriad experiences, reflections, and epiphanies we've encountered. It serves as a shield against societal pressures, defending us from the allure of conformity and the drizzles of self-doubt. Draped in this cloak, we find warmth in authenticity, courage in self-acceptance, and power in vulnerability. Wearing our truth is a bold declaration of self, a statement that while the world may ebb and flow around us, our core remains constant, genuine, and resolutely true to who we are.

The symphony of the universe resonates with count- less melodies, and my truth adds a harmonious note to its grand composition.

By honoring my unique song, I not only uplift myself but also amplify the collective chorus of authenticity that binds us all

In the vast orchestra of existence, every individual possesses a unique tune, a distinct contribution to the universal melody. By cherishing and expressing our individual truth, we enrich this collective symphony. Our authenticity, like a beautiful note, resonates within the vast expanse, touching others, inspiring them, and adding depth to the collective music. Embracing our unique song is not a solitary act; it's a powerful contribution to the chorus of genuine voices, fostering connection and unity in a world craving authentic expression.

My truth, though it may evolve and transform, is the bedrock upon which I build the edifice of my identity.

Its foundation is unshakeable, forged in the fires of self-discovery and acceptance. As I continue to explore, grow, and change, I remain anchored in the authenticity of who I am.

Truth, in its essence, serves as both the compass and foundation of our identity. While the outer layers of our being may change with time and experience, the core of our truth remains steadfast. This foundation, crafted through introspection, trials, and moments of profound realization, provides stability amidst the ever-evolving landscape of life. As we journey through different phases, embracing new insights and discarding outdated beliefs, our authentic self serves as the anchor, ensuring we never drift too far from our essence. This truth is the bedrock, the unyielding ground upon which the majestic structure of our identity proudly stands.

The brilliance of my truth is not dimmed by shadows of misunderstanding or judgment.

Like a lighthouse, it shines bright, cutting through the fog and leading me towards a life of integrity, love, and self-affirmation. My truth is my beacon, and by its light, I navigate the waters of existence.

Truth is a powerful force, unwavering and luminous, even when external forces attempt to eclipse its brilliance. Misunderstandings and judgments, though often external, can sometimes permeate our inner sanctum, casting doubts and clouds of uncertainty. Yet, our authentic truth, much like a steadfast lighthouse, continues to emit its radiant light. This light is not just a symbol of clarity but a guid-ing force that directs us on our path, ensuring we remain aligned with our core values, love, and self-acceptance. Navigating life's complexities may at times seem daunting, but with the beacon of our truth to guide us, we can steer our way with confidence, ensuring our journey remains true to our authentic selves.

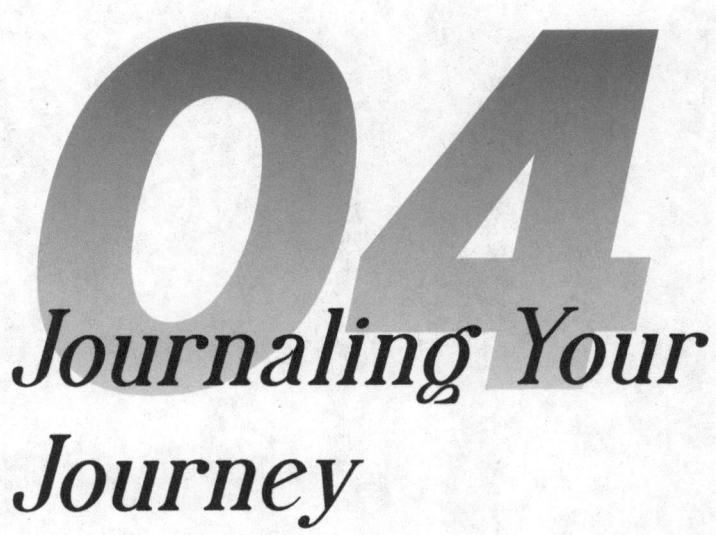

04
Journaling Your Journey

Self-Reflection: Dive Deep

understanding your thoughts, emotions, and behaviors

Journey Within

Think back to a moment in your life when you felt truly authentic. Describe that moment. What were the circumstances? How did it make you feel, and what can you learn from revisiting this memory?

Emotional Landscape

When you experience strong emotions, what triggers them most often? Write about a recent time when a particular event or interaction evoked a powerful emotional response. Dive deep into the layers of that emotion. Was it purely the surface emotion, or were there underlying feelings as well?

Behavioral Patterns

Reflect on a recurring behavior or habit of yours. Why do you think you've developed this pattern? Can you trace its origin to a particular event or series of events in your life? How does it serve or hinder you now?

Inner Dialogues

We all have an inner voice or voices. What does yours typically say? Is it supportive, critical, or perhaps a mix of both? Write a conversation between you and your inner voice, exploring its tone, content, and underlying intentions.

Dreams and Meanings

Have you had a dream recently that left a strong impression on you? Describe it in detail. What feelings did it evoke, and what symbolism or messages do you believe it might carry for you?

Dreams & Aspirations: Visioning Forward

explore your future goals, ambitions, and the life you envision for yourself

Vision Board in Words

If you were to create a vision board for the next five years, what would be on it? Describe the images, words, and feelings you would include, detailing the dreams you hope to achieve.

Conversations with Future Self

Imagine you're having a coffee date with your future self, ten years down the line. What would they tell you about the life you're leading? What achievements or experiences would they share? Write down the conversation.

Obstacles & Overcoming

What do you perceive as the biggest obstacle or challenge between you and your ultimate dream? Now, imagine a scenario where you overcome this hurdle. Describe the steps you took and how you felt.

Legacy Building

When you think about the legacy you want to leave behind, what comes to mind? What do you want to be remembered for, and what contributions or changes do you hope to make in the world or in the lives of those around you?

Day in the Dream Life

Detail a day in your dream life. From the moment you wake up to the time you go to bed, what does it look like? Where are you? Who are you with? What work or activities are you engaged in?

Past & Memory: Echoes of Yesterday

reflect on your past experiences, childhood memories, and the lessons they've taught you

Childhood Playground

Think back to your favorite place as a child—a playground, a relative's house, a secret hideout. Describe this place in vivid detail. What feelings does this memory evoke? Why do you think this place left such an imprint on your memory?

Influential Figures

Reflect on someone from your past who left a significant impact on you, for better or worse. Write about the moments you shared, the lessons they taught you, and how they've shaped the person you are today.

Life Chapters

If you were to divide your life into chapters, what would the titles be? Describe a key event or memory from each chapter and how it contributed to your growth or understanding of the world.

Letters Unsent

Is there something you wish you could've said to someone from your past but never did? Write that unsent letter now. It could be an apology, a thank you, or a simple sharing of feelings.

Lost and Found

Reflect on a time you felt lost—emotionally, physically, or spiritually. How did you find your way back? What resources or people helped guide you, and what did you discover about yourself in the process?

Relationships & Connections: Bonds & Bridges

understand your dynamics with family, friends, partners, and even acquaintances

Defining Moments

Think of a pivotal moment in a significant relationship—perhaps a turning point, a realization, or a shared experience. Describe the event and its aftermath. How did it change or solidify the dynamic between you and the other person?

The Roles We Play

Reflect on the different roles* you take on in various relationships (e.g., the caregiver, the listener, the motivator). Do you feel these roles truly represent who you are? Are there any roles you'd like to change or evolve?

*More information on roles can be found at the end in Part 6: Understanding the Spectrum.

Unspoken Words

*Is there something you've been holding back from saying to some-
one close to you? Explore the reasons behind your silence and how it
might feel to express those words, whether it's a confession, a griev-
ance, or a declaration.*

Connections Map

Create a mind map or web of the key people in your life. Draw lines connecting individuals who have relationships with each other. Reflect on the dynamics and intricacies of this web. Are there connections you wish to strengthen? Are there some that need reevaluation?

Lessons in Love

Consider a past relationship—romantic or otherwise—that ended. What lessons did you learn from that connection? How has it informed your approach to subsequent relationships?

Overcoming Challenges: Rising Above

understand your dynamics with family, friends, partners, and even acquaintances

Mountains Climbed

Recall a challenge you've faced and overcome in the past. Describe the situation, your feelings at the onset, the steps you took to address it, and how you felt once it was resolved. What strength or wisdom did you gain from that experience?

Facing Fears

List down three of your current fears. Dive into the root of each one. What can you do to confront and possibly overcome these fears? Are there actionable steps you can take?

The Roadblock

Reflect on a recent setback or disappointment. Instead of focusing on the negative, write about potential lessons or redirections this setback might be pointing you toward. How can this challenge be a disguised opportunity?

Your Support System

Who do you turn to when facing challenges? Describe a time when someone played a crucial role in helping you navigate a difficult situation. What did their support mean to you, and how did it shape the outcome?

The Art of Resilience

Think of a time when you had to bounce back from adversity. How did you rebuild or rejuvenate yourself? What coping mechanisms or rituals did you rely on?

Gratitude & Positivity: Light Within

highlight the things you're grateful for and the positive aspects of your life

Daily Blessings

At the end of each day for a week, list three things that brought you joy or for which you're grateful. Reflect on why these particular moments or things stood out amongst everything else.

Unexpected Gifts

Think of a time when something unexpectedly good happened to you. It could be a kind gesture, a lucky event, or a serendipitous meeting. How did it make you feel, and how has it influenced your perspective on life?

People of Positivity

Who in your life consistently uplifts you and brings positivity? Describe a specific instance when they made a significant positive impact on your day or life. What qualities of theirs do you admire most?

Silver Linings

Reflect on a challenging situation where you eventually found a silver lining or a positive takeaway. How did recognizing this aspect help you cope or view challenges differently?

Nature's Gratitude

Spend some time in nature, whether it's a park, a garden, or even just observing the sky from your window. Note down the things in nature you're grateful for and the feelings they evoke.

Creativity & Expression: Soul's Palette

dive into your passions, hobbies, and the ways you express your creativity

First Brushes with Creativity

Think back to one of your earliest memories of creating something, whether it was a drawing, a story, a song, or even a childhood game. Describe that creation. How did it make you feel, and how does it compare to how you express yourself now?

Passion Projects

What's a project or hobby you've always wanted to start but haven't yet? Detail what's holding you back and outline the first three steps you'd need to take to begin.

Creative Inspirations

Who or what inspires your creative side the most? It could be an artist, a family member, nature, music, or even a particular emotion. Describe why this source is so influential and how it sparks your creativity.

Artistic Evolution

Reflect on how your creative expression has changed over the years. Are there themes, styles, or mediums you've moved away from or embraced more deeply? What factors influenced these shifts?

Expression Blockade

Every creative individual faces blocks or periods of stagnation. Recall a time you felt blocked in your creativity. How did you navigate this period? If you're currently facing one, brainstorm ways you might break through.

Spirituality & Mindfulness: Finding Center

reflect on your beliefs, practices, and moments of
mindfulness or spiritual connection

Spiritual Roots

Reflect on the origins of your spiritual beliefs. How were they formed? Were they influenced by family traditions, personal experiences, or explorations into different philosophies and practices? How have they evolved over time?

Mindful Moments

Think back to a moment when you felt truly present—fully engaged with your surroundings, at peace, and connected. Describe the experience in detail. What can you do to cultivate more of these moments in your daily life?

Symbols and Signs

Are there certain symbols, rituals, or signs that hold spiritual significance for you? Detail their meanings and the comfort or guidance they provide.

Challenges to Belief

Recall a time when your beliefs were challenged, either by external factors or internal doubts. How did you navigate this period? What did you learn about your spiritual foundation through this experience?

Practices and Rituals

What daily or weekly practices do you engage in (or wish to engage in) that cultivate your sense of spirituality or mindfulness? This could range from meditation, prayer, nature walks, or even certain reading materials. Describe the impact they have on your well-being.

Nature & Environment: Earth's Embrace

explore your connection with the natural world, its impact on you, and your impact on it

Nature's Sanctuary

Recall a place in nature where you've felt most at peace—a forest, a beach, a mountaintop, or even a quiet garden. Describe this place in detail. How did it make you feel, and why do you think it had such a profound effect on you?

Nature's Lessons

Nature often mirrors life in many ways. Think of a time you witnessed something in nature—a changing season, the resilience of a plant, the flow of a river—that offered insight or reflection on a personal situation. What did you learn?

Human Footprint

Reflect on your personal impact on the environment. Are there habits or behaviors you could change to be more environmentally friendly? List actionable steps you can take to lessen your ecological footprint.

Wildlife Wonders

Think about an encounter you've had with a wild animal, whether it was a bird singing outside your window, a deer crossing your path, or even just observing creatures in their natural habitat. How did this experience make you feel about your place in the vast web of life?

Natural Healing

The natural world often offers healing in unexpected ways. Have you ever turned to nature for solace or recovery, be it through a walk in the woods, gardening, or simply sitting by a body of water? Describe the therapeutic effects it had on you.

Cultural & Societal Observations: The World Around

write about societal norms, cultural events, or your place within the larger world

Cultural Celebrations

Reflect on a cultural celebration or tradition that holds significance for you. Describe its origins, practices, and the personal meaning it carries. How does participating (or not participating) in this event shape your understanding of your own identity?

Questioning Norms

Think about a societal norm you've questioned or struggled with. Why do you think this norm exists? How does it affect you and others? Do you feel it should change, and if so, how?

Cultural Exposure

Describe a time when you experienced a culture vastly different from your own, either through travel, reading, or interaction with individuals. What surprised or challenged you? What did you learn from this exposure?

Societal Evolution

Consider how societal values and norms have shifted within your life-time. Which changes do you view positively, and which concern you? What do you believe influenced these shifts?

Your Place in the Mosaic

Everyone is a unique blend of various cultural, societal, and personal influences. Reflect on the different elements that make up your cultural and societal identity. How do these elements interact, conflict, or harmonize within you?

05

Insightful
Interludes

Quotes for Empowerment

Throughout history, individuals have risen to challenge norms, break barriers, and redefine societal boundaries. They've often done so using their voices, words that resonate and echo through time, leaving a lasting impact on generations. Within these pages, you'll find a curated collection of wisdom, wit, and insight from LGBTQ+ icons and allies, from trailblazers of the past to the luminaries of our current age.

These quotes aren't just words; they are declarations of truth, affirmations of identity, and celebrations of love in all its forms. They reflect the struggles faced, the victories won, and the indomitable spirit of the community.

As you journey through this section, let each quote be a source of inspiration, a beacon of hope, and a reminder of the strength that lies in authenticity. Whether you find solace in these words or are fueled by their fire, remember that every voice, including yours, is a vital thread in the rich tapestry of our shared experiences.

So, dear reader, let's dive into the minds and hearts of those who've walked paths similar and different, yet undeniably intertwined with ours. Let their words empower you, challenge you, and uplift you. After all, a single voice can inspire, but together, we create a chorus that can change the world.

Quotes for Empowerment

"

We deserve to experience love fully, equally, without shame, and without compromise. –Elliot Page

"

"

It is not our differences that divide us. It is our inability to recognize, accept, and celebrate those differences. –Audre Lorde

"

"

You have to go the way your blood beats. If you don't live the only life you have, you won't live some other life, you won't live any life at all. –James Baldwin

"

> Sometimes it is the people no one can imagine anything of, who do the things no one can imagine. –Alan Turing

> Being born gay, Black, and female is not a revolutionary act. Being proud to be a gay, Black female is. –Lena Waithe

> So let me be clear: I'm proud to be gay, and I consider being gay among the greatest gifts God has given me. –Tim Cook

66

There's nothing wrong with you. There's a lot wrong with the world you live in. –Chris Colfer

99

66

If you can't love yourself, how in the hell are you gonna love somebody else? –RuPaul

99

66

There's no right or wrong way to be gay. No right or wrong way to come out. It's your journey, do it the way you wanna do it. –Tan France

99

"

We have to be visible. We should not be ashamed of who we are. –Marsha P. Johnson

"

"

Every time a trans person comes out publicly, my heart leaps for joy. That kind of visibility is essential to progress. –Charlotte Clymer

"

"

Remember, bisexuality doesn't mean halfway between gay or straight. It is its own identity. –Evan Rachel Wood

"

Poetry Pages

In the vast mosaic of human expression, poetry stands as one of the most intimate and poignant forms of communication. It is in the carefully chosen words and the spaces between them that emotions breathe, thoughts crystallize, and identities take form. For the LGBTQ+ community, poetry has long been a refuge—a sacred space where love, struggles, joy, pain, and the myriad complexities of life are laid bare.

Over the ages, the quill of the poet has chronicled tales that are both universal and deeply personal. It's within these verses that individuals have sought to define themselves, confront societal norms, and dream of worlds where love is unchained from prejudice. LGBTQ+ themes within poetry aren't merely stories; they are testaments of existence, affirmations of identities that have, for too long, been silenced or side-lined.

Each poem, in its essence, is a journey. Some traverse the winding paths of self-discovery, others echo the heartbeats of lovers in stolen moments, and some are fierce roars against the injustices faced. They are chronicles of resilience in the face of discrimination, hymns of love that refuses to be bound, and ballads of hope for brighter tomorrows.

In this section, we aim to celebrate this rich tapestry of poetic expression from the LGBTQ+ community. From the gentle whispers of self-acceptance to the exuberant shouts of pride, these poems encapsulate the myriad experiences of a community that continues to shape and be shaped by its stories. As you delve into these pages, may you find reflections of your own experiences, insights into others', and above all, the comforting reminder that you are never alone in your feelings, struggles, or dreams.

In the days of unbridled dreams and cotton candy seams,
A secret self whispered, deep within my core,
Tiny inklings of something more,
Hide-and-seek in the chambers of my heart,
Hints of a journey, ready to start.

Childhood Reflections

From the shadows, I emerged, to light and open air,
Revealing my true colors, with layers stripped bare,
The weight of a secret, from my shoulders did fall,
Some cheered, some jeered, but I stood tall.
A journey of tears, laughter, and self-reveal,
My truth, my story, my heart did unseal.

Coming Out

A dance between binaries, stepping beyond,
Discovering realms where spirits respond,
Fluid, static, somewhere in between,
I sought my truth, in spaces unseen.
Neither this nor that, or perhaps both, indeed,
In the vast spectrum, I sowed my seed.

Gender Exploration

Words can confine, yet also define,
Labels bestowed, both theirs and mine,
A name for the feelings, a box for the soul,
Yet, I am more than parts, I am whole.
Beyond mere tags, my spirit does soar,
Infinite, boundless, forever more.

Labels & Beyond

LGBTQ hues, blended with shades of my skin,
My culture, my race, the battles therein.
At crossroads of identity, I stand proud and tall,
For in every facet, I give it my all.
Each intersection, a tale unique,
The confluence of paths, the strength I seek.

Intersectionality

Face to face, in silvery reflection,
I posed hard questions, sought direction.
"Who are you?" whispered the me in the glass,
With every answer, I found impasse.
Yet, over time, in those silent chats,
I found my essence, beyond the stats.

Mirror Conversations

In the echoes of time, voices resound,
Ancestors who fought, their spirits unbound.
They paved the paths, broke barriers wide,
In their legacy, I take immense pride.
For every right, every freedom I see,
I honor those who made it be.

Legacy & Ancestors

Whispers of passion, in fleeting glance,
The delicate waltz, that first dance.
Hearts fluttering, like caged doves,
Such is the magic of first loves.
But with sweet joy, sometimes comes pain,
Yet the allure of firsts, will ever remain.

First Loves

Echoes of laughter, shadows of touch,
Memories of lovers who meant so much.
Time marches forward, but moments stay still,
Reminders of spaces they used to fill.
Though they've moved on, in heart they reside,
As lessons learned, in life's vast tide.

Lovers Lost

Hidden alleyways, shadows cast long,
Whispered I love yous, a secret song.
Hands brushing hands, in the dark of the night,
Stolen moments, out of sight.
In a world not always kind or fair,
These clandestine meetings, a breath of fresh air.

Stolen Moments

Rainbows of passion, spectrum wide,
Love in every hue, side by side.
Reds of passion, blues of trust,
Every shade of love, vibrant and just.
For love knows no boundaries, it's free,
Celebrating love in its vast diversity.

Love in Color

With every wrinkle, love did grow,
In the eyes of youth, old passions glow.
A dance of ages, young and old,
Stories of love, timelessly retold.
For love doesn't count the passing years,
It simply grows, through joys and tears.

Age & Love

Through seasons changing, and hair turning grey,
In silent understanding, they make their way.
Years of togetherness, through thick and thin,
Growing together, from within.
Chronicles of trust, partnership so fine,
Celebrating bonds, that with time, shine.

Long-Term Bonds

To be seen, to be known, for all that I am,
In the warmth of embrace, without any sham.
To love and be loved, in authenticity,
Is the purest joy, in vast entirety.
For when love meets acceptance, hearts take flight,
In the bliss of being, everything feels right.

Love & Acceptance

Against a tide of murmured disdain,
We stand, unyielding, amidst the rain.
For every sneer and every slight,
We rise, radiant, shining bright.
Though society may try to confine,
Our spirit breaks every line.

Battles with Society

In the mirror, confronting the foe,
The harshest critic I've come to know.
Battles raging, within heart's hall,
But with every fall, I stand tall.
For the journey to love the self,
Is the most invaluable wealth.

Inner Demons

With banners raised and voices loud,
Emerging from the silenced crowd.
For every injustice, we unite and stand,
Marching together, hand in hand.
In the face of adversity, we resist and persist,
Ensuring our rights always exist.

Activism & Protests

In the quiet aftermath of a storm,
Seeking warmth, seeking to transform.
Heart's wounds, time might seal,
Yet memories remain, so real.
But in the tapestry of pain and despair,
Threads of hope weave repair.

Loss & Healing

Steps of progress, big and small,
Collective efforts, answering the call.
For every hurdle, every stony path,
We've known joy, we've known wrath.
But with every milestone we cross,
We reclaim what was once lost.

Achievements & Milestones

To those who stand beside, unwavering, true,
Our gratitude is endless, our bond anew.
But to foes who challenge, at every bend,
We confront with grace, our truth won't bend.
For in the dance of support and disdain,
Our resolve only stands to gain.

Allies & Adversaries

In the labyrinth of the mind, we tread,
Seeking solace, often led by dread.
But even in the darkest, trying hour,
We find strength, an inner power.
Acknowledging pain, yet seeking the light,
For mental well-being, we continue the fight.

Mental Health

Colors cascade, emotions rise,
Underneath the vast open skies.
Pride's parade, joyous and bold,
Tales of love and courage, retold.
A celebration, a statement so clear,
We're here, we're proud, year after year.

Pride Celebrations

In corners where acceptance thrives,
Where love is love, and life truly arrives.
These safe havens, where souls are bare,
Warmth and understanding, beyond compare.
Here, hearts beat in a synchronized tone,
No one is ever truly alone.

Safe Havens

Beyond romance, a bond so profound,
In friendships, true riches are found.
In laughter, in tears, in moments small,
Steadfast friends stand tall.
Within the community, these ties bind,
Heart to heart, mind to mind.

Friendships

Brick by brick, hand in hand,
Together, we make a stand.
In unity, strength does reside,
Community building, our collective pride.
For every effort, every shared goal,
Uplifts and heals the collective soul.

Community Building

Whispers of shared joys, tears,
Resonating through the years.
Stories that touch, stories that move,
In every recount, we find our groove.
In this vast community's shared song,
We find where our tales belong.

Shared Stories

Beyond blood, beyond birth-given ties,
Chosen families, under the skies.
Where love defines, and hearts align,
In these families, stars truly shine.
Together we create, together we care,
An unbreakable bond, beyond compare.

LGBTQ+ Families

For those who walked before our time,
Whose stories became the paradigm.
To those we've lost, but not in vain,
Your legacy, forever will remain.
In every step we take today,
We honor you, in every way.

Legacy

In the stillness of the night, a dream takes flight,
A world where love is met with pure delight.
Beyond prejudice, beyond hate's door,
Equality reigns, forevermore.

Dreams of Equality

For the ones who follow our stride,
May they walk with heads held high in pride.
Dreams untethered, spirits free,
The future is theirs, as bright as can be.

Youth & Future Generations

In pixels and codes, our stories unfold,
Digital tales, courageously told.
The age of tech shapes our quest,
Uniting voices from East to West.

Technological Impact

From distant shores to lands we know,
The winds of change continually blow.
Rights recognized, love takes its place,
Progress marches, a worldwide embrace.

Global Movements

Through brushstrokes, lyrics, scenes on screens,
Future visions, in myriad means.
Art guides us, makes hopes shine bright,
A beacon leading through the darkest night.

Artistic Expressions

06
Understanding the Spectrum

Descriptions of LGBTQ+ Identities

- **Lesbian:** Women who are attracted to other women, either romantically, emotionally, or sexually.

- **Gay:** Typically, men who are attracted to other men, either romantically, emotionally, or sexually. However, the term can also be used broadly to describe same-sex attraction.

- **Bisexual (Bi):** Individuals who are attracted to both men and women. This attraction doesn't have to be equally split and can vary in intensity.

- **Transgender (Trans):** People whose gender identity differs from the sex they were assigned at birth. It's important to note that being transgender does not imply any specific sexual orientation.

- **Queer:** Historically, this was a derogatory slang term used to identify LGBTQ+ people. It has been reclaimed by many in the LGBTQ+ community and is often used as an umbrella term for anyone not strictly heterosexual or cisgender.

- **Questioning:** People who are exploring their sexuality or gender identity and have not yet chosen a definitive label.

- **Intersex:** Individuals born with physical sex characteristics that don't fit typical definitions of male or female.

- **Non-Binary (NB):** People who don't identify as exclusively male or female. They may view themselves as both, neither, or on a spectrum.

- **Asexual (Ace):** People who experience little to no sexual attraction to others. They might still have romantic feelings without a desire for sexual activity.

- **Pansexual (Pan):** Individuals attracted to people of any gender or gender identity.

- **Genderfluid:** People whose gender identity changes over time. They might identify as male, female, both, or neither at different times.

- **Two-Spirit:** A term used by some Indigenous North American cultures to describe a person who embodies both masculine and feminine spirits.

- **Demisexual:** People who only experience sexual attraction after forming a deep emotional connection.

- **Cisgender (Cis):** People whose gender identity aligns with the sex they were assigned at birth.

- **Aromantic (Aro):** People who experience little to no romantic attraction, regardless of sexual attraction.

Note: The LGBTQ+ community is vast and evolving, and labels and definitions may change or be expanded upon over time. Always approach individuals with respect and openness, recognizing the importance of self-identification.

Pronouns: Importance & Respect

What Are Pronouns?

Pronouns are words we use to refer to someone without using their name. Common pronouns include "*he*", "*she*", and "*they*". However, the range of pronouns people identify with is vast and varied.

Why Are Pronouns Important?

- **Affirmation:** Using correct pronouns validates and respects a person's identity.

- **Inclusivity:** It creates an environment where all individuals, regardless of gender identity, feel welcome and seen.

- **Prevention of Harm:** Misgendering, or using incorrect pronouns, can perpetuate feelings of dysphoria and alienation in transgender and non-binary individuals.

Common Pronouns & How to Use Them:

- **He/Him/His:** He is a writer. This book is his. It belongs to him.

- **She/Her/Hers:** She is a writer. This book is hers. It belongs to her.

- **They/Them/Theirs:** They are a writer. This book is theirs. It belongs to them.

- **Ze/Hir/Hirs:** Ze is a writer. This book is hirs. It belongs to hir.

- **Ey/Em/Eirs:** Ey is a writer. This book is eirs. It belongs to em.

Note: There are many pronouns people might identify with. This is just a short list of examples.

Asking & Using Pronouns Respectfully:

- **Introduce with Pronouns:** *"Hi, I'm Alex and my pronouns are they/them."* This sets a tone of respect and awareness.

- **Ask Politely:** If unsure, it's okay to ask: *"Can you share your pronouns? I want to make sure I address you correctly."*

- **Correct Mistakes:** If you slip up, correct yourself, apologize briefly, and move on. Over-apologizing can shift the focus to your feelings instead of the person you misgendered.

- **Educate Others:** If you hear someone else use the wrong pronoun, gently correct them.

Using Multiple Pronouns:

Some individuals may identify with more than one set of pronouns. For example, someone might use both *"she"* and *"they"* pronouns interchangeably. In such cases, it's respectful to alternate between the sets of pronouns the person has identified with or use the specific one they have indicated for that particular context or setting.

Final Thought:

Pronouns are more than just grammar – they are an essential aspect of an individual's identity. By asking and using the correct pronouns, we show respect, create inclusive spaces, and contribute to the overall well-being of our diverse community.

Glossary of Terms (Beyond the Basics)

- **Agender:** People who do not identify with any gender. They may feel genderless or may feel that they do not fit into the binary genders of male and female.

- **Ally:** Someone who supports and stands up for the rights of LGBTQ+ people even though they may not identify as LGBTQ+ themselves.

- **Bigender:** People who identify as having two genders, either simultaneously or varying between them.

- **Cishet:** An abbreviation for cisgender heterosexual, referring to someone who both identifies with the sex they were assigned at birth and is attracted to the opposite sex.

- **Closeted/In the Closet:** Refers to an LGBTQ+ individual who has not disclosed their sexuality or gender identity to others.

- **Coming Out:** The process of self-acceptance and disclosure to others about one's LGBTQ+ identity.

- **Deadnaming:** Referring to a transgender person using their birth name instead of their chosen name.

- **Drag King/Queen:** Individuals who perform and express as the opposite gender, often for entertainment. This doesn't necessarily reflect their day-to-day gender identity or sexual orientation.

- **Gender Dysphoria:** A profound distress resulting from the incongruence between one's gender identity and their assigned sex at birth.

- **Gender Expression:** How one expresses their gender identity, often through behavior, clothing, hairstyle, or voice.

- **Gender Non-Conforming (GNC):** Individuals whose gender expression does not fit societal norms for their assigned sex.

- **Genderqueer:** A term for people who reject traditional gender distinctions and identify as neither exclusively male nor exclusively female. It's an umbrella term that can encompass a variety of gender identities.

- **Heteronormative:** A viewpoint that expresses heterosexuality as the norm or default sexual orientation, which can result in stigmatizing or marginalizing LGBTQ+ identities.

- **Homophobia:** The fear, hatred, or discrimination towards homosexuals or LGBTQ+ identities.

- **Misgender:** Referring to someone using a word, especially a pronoun or form of address, which does not correctly reflect the gender with which they identify.

- **Polysexual:** Attracted to many, but not necessarily all, genders.

- **Skoliosexual:** Attracted to non-binary and genderqueer people.

- **Transphobia:** The fear, hatred, or discrimination towards transgender or gender non-conforming people.

- **Biphobia:** The fear, hatred, or discrimination specifically towards bisexual individuals. This can manifest in various ways, such as questioning the validity of bisexuality, making assumptions about promiscuity, or suggesting that bisexuality is just a "phase."

- **Bi-Erasure (or Bisexual Erasure):** The tendency to ignore, remove, falsify, or re-explain evidence of bisexuality in history, academia, news media, and other primary sources. In a broader context, it's the denial or dismissal of the existence of bisexuality altogether. This contributes to the invisibility of bisexual identities in society and can lead to feelings of isolation among bisexual individuals.

Biphobia & Bi-Erasure: A Closer Look

Biphobia:

Biphobia is the fear, hatred, or prejudice against bisexual individuals. It manifests in a variety of ways, from overt discrimination to subtle comments that invalidate a bisexual person's experience. Like other forms of prejudice, biphobia is rooted in misunderstanding, ignorance, or fear of the unknown.

Examples of Biphobic Statements:

- *"It's just a phase."*
- *"You're just confused."*
- *"You're greedy."*
- *"Pick a side!"*

Bi-Erasure:

Bi-erasure (or bisexual erasure) refers to the tendency to ignore, remove, falsify, or re-explain evidence of bisexuality in history, academia, news media, and other primary sources. In more everyday contexts, it can be the simple denial of the existence of bisexuality altogether or the assumption that a person's current partner determines their sexuality.

Effects of Bi-Erasure:

- **Invisibility:** Many bisexual individuals feel that they don't fit neatly into the "*gay*" or "*straight*" world, leading to feelings of isolation.

- **Invalidation:** It denies the genuine feelings and experiences of bisexual individuals.

- **Mental Health:** Due to the stress of feeling invisible or invalidated, many bisexual people can experience mental health challenges.

Why It Matters:

Addressing biphobia and bi-erasure is crucial for several reasons.

By acknowledging bisexuality and the valid experiences of bisexual individuals, we:

- **Support Mental Health:** Recognizing and validating bisexual identities can reduce feelings of isolation and confusion.

- **Promote Inclusivity:** It ensures that all LGBTQ+ community members are acknowledged and celebrated.

- **Educate & Dispel Myths:** Combatting bi-erasure and biphobia educates society at large, dispelling misconceptions about bisexuality.

What Can You Do?

- **Listen Actively:** If someone tells you they're bisexual, believe them.

- **Educate Yourself:** Read, watch, and learn more about bisexuality and the challenges faced by bisexual individuals.

- **Challenge Biphobic Comments:** If you hear someone making an inappropriate comment, challenge them and inform them about why it's hurtful.

- **Spread Awareness:** Share articles, documentaries, or personal stories that shed light on biphobia and bi-erasure.

By shining a light on these issues, we can hope to pave the way for greater acceptance, understanding, and validation of the bisexual community within the broader LGBTQ+ spectrum and society at large.

Trans Awareness & Understanding: A Closer Look

Transphobia:

Transphobia encompasses a range of negative attitudes, feelings, or actions toward transgender or transsexual individuals. It can manifest as disdain, aversion, prejudice, or even violence. Often, transphobia is rooted in fear, misunderstanding, or a strict belief in a gender binary, which doesn't accommodate the full spectrum of gender identities.

Examples of Transphobic Statements or Actions:

- Deliberately misgendering someone or using their dead-name.

- *"What's your real name?"* or *"What were you born as?"*

- Joking about or belittling gender transition.

- Refusing to accept the identity of a trans individual unless they've undergone surgery.

Erasure of Trans Histories:

Many trans individuals have played significant roles throughout history, but their contributions and identities are often downplayed or overlooked. In contemporary media, trans narratives can be simplified, stereotyped, or entirely left out.

Effects of Trans Erasure:

- **Invisibility:** Trans individuals can feel as though their experiences and identities aren't valid or acknowledged.

- **Mental & Physical Health Risks:** Lack of representation combined with direct discrimination can lead to significant health disparities.

- **Loss of History:** By not recognizing trans individuals in history, we lose a richer understanding of the past.

Why It Matters:

Promoting understanding and combating transphobia and erasure is imperative for several reasons:

- **Human Rights:** Trans individuals deserve the same rights, respect, and dignity as anyone else.

- **Mental & Physical Wellbeing:** Understanding and acceptance can directly reduce the mental health disparities seen in the trans community.

- **Broader Societal Benefits:** When trans individuals are supported and understood, society benefits from their contributions without being hindered by prejudice.

What Can You Do?

- **Educate Yourself:** Seek out resources to better understand the trans experience.

- **Listen & Respect:** When trans individuals share their stories or correct you on pronouns, listen and show respect.

- **Challenge Transphobic Remarks:** Stand up against derogatory jokes, comments, or misconceptions.

- **Advocate:** Support trans rights in your community and beyond, whether it's supporting trans-inclusive policies or joining local advocacy efforts.

Understanding and supporting the trans community is not only about combating prejudice but about enriching society as a whole. When we celebrate and support all members of our community, we create a more inclusive, understanding, and diverse world.

Microaggressions: General

What are Microaggressions?

Microaggressions are subtle, often unintentional, comments or actions that express bias or prejudice towards a marginalized group. These remarks can be based on race, gender, sexual orientation, or any other characteristic. In the context of the LGBTQ+ community, microaggressions often reflect underlying societal norms and assumptions about gender and sexuality.

Examples of Microaggressions towards LGBTQ+ Individuals:

- **Assuming Heterosexuality:** Asking a woman about her boyfriend or a man about his girlfriend without knowing their sexual orientation.

- **Gender Binaries:** Saying things like "boys will be boys" or "you throw like a girl" enforces traditional gender roles.

- **Misunderstanding Bisexuality:** Statements like "It's just a phase" or "So you're half gay, half straight?"

- **Trivializing Identity:** Referring to someone's pronouns or gender transition as a "preference" or "lifestyle choice."

- **Inappropriate Curiosity:** Asking invasive questions about someone's anatomy, surgery status, or how they have sex.

- **Tokenizing:** Saying things like "You're my gay best friend!" or using someone as a representative for their entire community.

- **Erasure:** "I never would've guessed you're LGBTQ+! You don't look it."

Why Microaggressions are Harmful:

While they might seem minor in isolation, the cumulative impact of microaggressions can be profound.

Constantly facing such comments can:

- **Diminish Self-Worth:** Continual invalidation can lead to feelings of being less than or not belonging.

- **Cause Mental Strain:** Constantly needing to address or internalize these comments can be mentally exhausting.

- **Reinforce Stereotypes:** Even unintentionally, these comments perpetuate societal stereotypes.

- **Isolate Individuals:** Making someone feel they don't belong can lead to isolation and reluctance to engage with certain communities or spaces.

How to Address and Reduce Microaggressions:

- **Educate Yourself:** Awareness of what microaggressions are is the first step to eliminating them.

- **Listen Actively:** If someone tells you that your comment was inappropriate or hurtful, listen without getting defensive.

- **Apologize:** If you realize you've made a microaggressive comment, a sincere apology can go a long way.

- **Challenge Microaggressions:** If you witness microaggressions, call them out (if it's safe to do so). This not only supports the person on the receiving end but also educates the person making the comment.

- **Seek Feedback:** Regularly asking for feedback and being open to it can help you become more self-aware.

Microaggressions can be deeply ingrained in our language and behaviors. Recognizing them, understanding their impact, and taking steps to reduce them is crucial for fostering a more inclusive and respectful environment for everyone.

Microaggressions: Within the LGBTQ+ Community

What are Intra-Community Microaggressions?

Even within the LGBTQ+ community, which is often considered a space of acceptance and understanding, subtle prejudices can exist. Intra-community microaggressions are those comments or behaviors that reveal biases or misunderstandings between different groups or identities within the LGBTQ+ umbrella.

Examples of Intra-Community Microaggressions:

- **Bisexual Dismissal:** Comments like "You're just confused" or "Pick a side."

- **Erasing Non-Binary Identities:** Statements such as "There are only two genders" or "It's just male and female, everything else is made up."

- **Minimizing Asexual/Aromantic Experiences:** Phrases like "You just haven't met the right person yet" or "Everyone feels that way sometimes."

- **Gatekeeping Trans Experiences:** Telling someone they aren't "trans enough" or questioning their decision not to pursue specific medical treatments.

- **Prioritizing Visible Identities:** Imposing a hierarchy where certain identities (often those that are most visible or commonly recognized) are seen as more "valid" or "important."

- **Assuming Homonormativity:** Expecting everyone in the LGBTQ+ community to fit a certain mold, for instance, assuming all gay men are effeminate or all lesbian women are masculine.

Creating a truly inclusive LGBTQ+ community requires recognizing and addressing the subtle tensions that might exist Through empathy, and education, the community can grow stronger and more united.

Types of Relationships & The Roles We Play

Types of Relationships:

- **Familial Relationships:** These are the bonds we share with our family members – parents, siblings, extended family, and chosen family.

- **Romantic Relationships:** Connections that are characterized by emotional and often physical intimacy. These can be short-term or lifelong, monogamous or polyamorous.

- **Platonic Friendships:** Non-romantic relationships where two people share mutual affection. Friends can be close confidants, casual acquaintances, or anything in between.

- **Professional Relationships:** The relationships we form at our workplaces or in professional settings, including with colleagues, bosses, mentors, and mentees.

- **Casual Acquaintances:** People we interact with occasionally, perhaps at social gatherings, clubs, or community events.

Roles We Often Play in Relationships:

- **The Caregiver:** Takes on a nurturing role, always looking out for the well-being of the other.

- **The Listener:** Offers an empathetic ear, always ready to listen without necessarily offering solutions.

- **The Motivator:** Pushes others to achieve their best, offering encouragement and sometimes tough love.

- **The Advisor:** Offers guidance and wisdom, helping others navigate challenges.

- **The Protector:** Looks out for potential harms or threats to loved ones, sometimes even at their own expense.

It's essential to understand that these roles are fluid. One might find themselves as the "Listener" in one relationship and the "Motivator" in another. It's also perfectly natural for roles to evolve or change over time as relationships grow and change.

Luminaries of the LGBTQ+ Community

from trailblazers of yesteryears to modern-day icons

Marsha P. Johnson
(1945-1992)

A prominent figure in the ear-ly days of the LGBTQ+ rights movement, Marsha P. Johnson was a black transgender woman who played a pivotal role in the events of the Stonewall Uprising in 1969. A fearless advocate for the rights of trans and queer people of color, Johnson co-founded the Street Transvestite (now Transgender) Action Revolutionaries (STAR) along-side Sylvia Rivera, providing support for homeless queer youth.

Sylvia Rivera
(1951-2002)

Rivera, a Venezuelan-Puerto Rican transgender activist, alongside Marsha P. Johnson, became a crucial voice for the rights of transgender and gender-nonconforming individ-uals. She was known for her tireless activism, advocating especially for the inclusion of transgender issues in the broader LGBTQ+ rights movement.

Harvey Milk
(1930-1978)

Harvey Milk made history as the first openly gay elected official in California when he won a seat on the San Francisco Board of Supervisors in 1977. Despite his short political career, curtailed by assassination, his legacy lives on as a symbol of progress, hope, and the fight for LGBTQ+ rights.

Audre Lorde
(1934-1992)

Audre Lorde was a self-pro-claimed "black, lesbian, mother, warrior, poet." Through her powerful writings, she tackled issues related to racism, feminism, and queer identity, creating a lasting legacy that continues to influence intersectional activism today.

James Baldwin
(1924-1987)

An iconic writer, James Bald-win's works, such as "Giovanni's Room" and "Go Tell It on the Mountain," grapple with themes of race, sexuality, and personal identity. His eloquent writings and speeches provided profound insights into the complexities of race and sexuality in America.

RuPaul Andre Charles
(1960-present)

RuPaul, a drag queen, actor, and recording artist, has brought drag culture to mainstream audiences worldwide, especially with the hit reality show *"RuPaul's Drag Race."* As a fierce advocate for self-expression and authenticity, RuPaul's mantra, *"If you can't love yourself, how in the hell are you gonna love somebody else?'* resonates with many.

Laverne Cox
(1972-present)

Breaking barriers as a trans actress, Laverne Cox shot to fame with her role in *"Orange Is the New Black."* She uses her platform to advocate for transgender rights and representation in media, paving the way for future trans actors.

Billy Porter
(1969-present)

A multi-talented actor, singer, and style icon, Billy Porter gained widespread acclaim for his role in the TV series *"Pose."* Unapologetically himself, Porter frequently challenges gender norms and societal expectations both on-screen and off.

Michaela Jaé Rodriguez
(1991-present)

As Blanca Rodriguez-Evangelista in the groundbreaking series "*Pose*," Michaela Jaé Rodriguez's portrayal of a trans woman of color in New York's ballroom scene has been nothing short of revolutionary. Off-screen, she continues to champion for transgender rights and representation.

Troye Sivan
(1995-present)

Troye Sivan Mellet quickly rose to prominence first as a YouTuber and then as a musician. Troye publicly came out as gay in 2013 via a YouTube video and has since been a vocal advocate for LGBTQ+ rights. His music often touches on themes of love, queer identity, and the challenges and joys of youth. Hits like "Youth" and "My My My!" have solidified his place as one of pop music's most promising voices.

Your Place in History

In the vast mosaic of LGBTQ+ history, each individual, each story, and each heartbeat adds depth, color, and context. You are not just a fleeting moment in this timeline but a pivotal chapter, weaving your own narrative into the larger fabric. Every tear, every laugh, every hurdle you've overcome, and every joy you've felt paints a unique stroke in this ever-evolving masterpiece. By standing in your truth, by letting your voice resonate, and by daring to live authentically, you etch your name in the annals of LGBTQ+ legacy.

Your journey, your resilience, your very existence champions the idea of a world where love, acceptance, and freedom reign supreme. As you add your photo to this collection, remember: you are not just witnessing history—you are making it, and future generations will look back with gratitude for the trails you've blazed. Welcome to the tapestry.

Welcome to your legacy.

YOUR PHOTO HERE

Name: _____

DOB: _____/_____/_____

BIO: _____

_____

_____

_____

_____

_____

_____

_____

_____

_____

Historical Highlights

a detailed timeline of LGBTQ+ milestones

1924
The Society for Human Rights in Chicago

In 1924, Chicago witnessed the birth of The Society for Human Rights, making it the first known gay rights organization in the U.S. Spearheaded by Henry Gerber, it aimed to provide a safe platform for dialogue and understanding for homosexuals. Unfortunately, due to societal pressures, its lifespan was short, enduring only a few months. Still, its mere existence served as a testament to the resilience and determination of the early LGBTQ+ community, marking the start of an enduring movement.

1969
The Stonewall Riots in New York City

Late June 1969 saw a series of spontaneous protests and violent confrontations between police and gay rights activists outside the Stonewall Inn, a gay bar in New York City. Sparked by frequent police raids and subsequent arrests, the Stonewall Riots became a catalyst for LGBTQ+ activism. These events inspired the formation of numerous gay rights organizations, and it is here that the foundations for modern LGBTQ+ rights movements were solidified.

1970
First Gay Pride Parades

In a powerful response to the Stonewall Riots the previous year, 1970 witnessed the inception of the Gay Pride parades in New York City, Los Angeles, and San Francisco. These events were not just parades but were protests against decades of oppression and an assertion of LGBTQ+ rights and visibility. Over time, these parades would grow in magnitude, reflecting the community's growing strength and solidarity.

1973
Declassification of Homosexuality as a Mental Disorder

In 1924, Chicago witnessed the birth of The Society for Human Rights, making it the first known gay rights organization in the U.S. Spearheaded by Henry Gerber, it aimed to provide a safe platform for dialogue and understanding for homosexuals. Unfortunately, due to societal pressures, its lifespan was short, enduring only a few months. Still, its mere existence served as a testament to the resilience and determination of the early LGBTQ+ community, marking the start of an enduring movement.

1977
Harvey Milk & Political Representation

Harvey Milk was elected to the San Francisco Board of Super-visors, making him one of the first openly gay elected officials in U.S. history. His tenure was tragically short-lived as he was assassinated in 1978. Milk's activism and representation broke barriers, and his legacy has continued to inspire generations of LGBTQ+ activists.

1980s
Emergence of the AIDS Crisis

The 1980s saw the rise of a devastating epidemic: AIDS. Misin-formation and prejudice ran rampant, with many initially deem-ing it the "gay plague." The crisis spurred the LGBTQ+ communi-ty into activism, leading to the establishment of organizations like ACT UP in 1987, which sought to bring about legislative and medical changes to address the crisis, combating both the disease and the systemic discrimination that accompanied it.

1982

Wisconsin Bans Discrimination

Wisconsin became the first U.S. state to outlaw discrimination on the basis of sexual orientation, a crucial step in acknowledging the rights of the LGBTQ+ community at the legislative level.

1993

"Don't Ask, Don't Tell" in the U.S. Military

Introduced as a compromise measure in 1993, "Don't Ask, Don't Tell" (DADT) prohibited military personnel from discriminating against or harassing closeted LGBTQ+ service members or applicants. However, it also barred openly gay or bisexual individuals from military service. This policy was a contentious issue in the U.S., reflecting the nation's broader struggle with LGBTQ+ rights, until its eventual repeal in 2011.

1998

Matthew Shepard's Death and Legacy

Matthew Shepard, a gay student, was brutally murdered in Wyoming. His death became a symbol of the violence faced by the LGBTQ+ community. In 2009, President Obama signed the Matthew Shepard and James Byrd, Jr. Hate Crimes Prevention Act into law, extending the definition of hate crimes to include those perpetrated because of a victim's sexuality or gender identity.

2000

Vermont Legalizes Civil Unions

At the dawn of the new millennium, Vermont became the pioneer U.S. state to legalize civil unions for same-sex couples, offering rights and responsibilities parallel to marriage. This landmark decision marked a crucial shift toward broader acceptance and equality for LGBTQ+ relationships.

2004
First U.S. State Legalizes Same-Sex Marriage

Massachusetts became the first U.S. state to legalize same-sex marriage, offering LGBTQ+ couples a recognition previously denied to them. This move paved the way for other states to follow suit in subsequent years.

2008
California's Proposition 8

California passed Proposition 8, a controversial amendment that defined marriage as between a man and a woman, thereby banning same-sex marriages. It was later deemed unconstitutional, but not before sparking widespread protests and bringing national attention to the issue of marriage equality.

2011
End of the U.S. Military's "Don't Ask, Don't Tell"

President Barack Obama signed a landmark law that would bring about the end of the "Don't Ask, Don't Tell" policy in the U.S. military, allowing LGBTQ+ members to openly serve.

2012
Tammy Baldwin Makes History

Tammy Baldwin, from Wisconsin, became the first openly gay politician to be elected to the U.S. Senate, marking a significant milestone in LGBTQ+ representation in politics.

2015
Nationwide Legalization of Same-Sex Marriage

In a monumental ruling, the U.S. Supreme Court declared in Obergefell v. Hodges that same-sex couples had the fundamental right to marry. This 5-4 decision eradicated any state bans on same-sex marriage, ensuring that love prevailed over prejudice, and making marriage equality the law of the land.

2016
Protection for Transgender Students

The Obama administration issued guidance declaring that public schools should allow transgender students to use bathrooms that match their gender identity, marking a significant step forward for transgender rights, although it faced considerable pushback and was later rescinded by the Trump administration.

2016
National Monuments & LGBTQ+ History

In June, then-President Barack Obama designated the Stonewall Inn in New York City as the first national monument to LGBTQ+ rights. The Stonewall National Monument encompasses Christopher Park and the surrounding area where the 1969 Stonewall uprising took place, an event widely considered the catalyst for the modern LGBTQ+ rights movement.

2017
Transgender Military Service Ban

In July, President Donald Trump announced via Twitter that he would reverse Obama-era policies and prohibit transgender individuals from serving in the U.S. military "in any capacity." The announcement and subsequent policy shift sparked widespread controversy and was challenged in the courts. Although various courts issued injunctions against implementing the ban, it ultimately went into effect in 2019.

2019

U.S. Protection Against Workplace Discrimination

In a landmark decision in June, the U.S. Supreme Court ruled in the Bostock v. Clayton County case that Title VII of the Civil Rights Act of 1964, which prohibits discrimination on the basis of sex, also covers discrimination based on sexual orientation and gender identity. This was a significant victory for LGBTQ+ rights, ensuring that individuals could not be fired from their jobs due to their sexuality or gender identity.

2019

World Health Organization's Classification

The World Health Organization (WHO) declassified being transgender as a mental disorder, recognizing the inherent human rights of transgender individuals and further challenging the stigmatization they face.

2020
U.S. Health Protections - Transgender

In June 2020, the Trump administration finalized a rule that
would remove nondiscrimination protections for LGBTQ+ individuals when it comes to health care and health insurance. This
change sought to erase Obama-era protections that had expanded the definition of sex discrimination to include discrimination based on gender identity. The rule was met with backlash
and legal challenges.

2020
Poland's "LGBT-Free Zones"

Throughout 2020, several towns and regions in Poland declared
themselves "LGBT-Free Zones," passing resolutions against
"LGBT propaganda." These actions drew international condem-
nation, including from the European Union, which responded
by withholding funding to certain Polish towns due to their
discriminatory policies.

2021

U.S. Executive Order on Gender Identity and Sexual Orientation

Shortly after taking office in January 2021, President Joe Biden signed an executive order emphasizing that every individual should be treated with respect and dignity and be able to live without fear, regardless of their gender identity or sexual orientation. The order directed agencies to enforce Title VII of the Civil Rights Act of 1964 and other laws that prohibit discrimination on the basis of gender identity or sexual orientation.

2021

Hungary's Anti-LGBTQ+ Legislation

In June 2021, Hungary's parliament passed a law banning all educational programs and materials for children that discuss homosexuality or transgender issues, framing it as a measure to protect children. The legislation, likened to Russia's "gay propaganda" law, was widely criticized by EU leaders, human rights groups, and the wider international community for infringing on the rights of LGBTQ+ individuals.

2021

Recognition of Non-Binary Gender in New Zealand

In March 2021, New Zealand approved a decision allowing the use of the gender indicator 'X' in passports. This decision was a significant step forward for non-binary and gender-diverse individuals, providing an option other than the binary 'M' (male) or 'F' (female) on official documents.

Present Day
Continuing Struggles and Triumphs

The timeline of LGBTQ+ rights, from its nascent movements in the early 20th century to the present day, paints a complex picture of resilience, community, and the continuous pursuit of equality. It is evident that tremendous strides have been made in the fight for rights and recognition. Historic verdicts, the establishment of protective legislation, and societal acceptance in many parts of the world bear testimony to this progress.

However, this journey has never been linear. Just as advancements are made, there are forces that attempt to reverse them, reminding us that the pursuit of equality is ongoing. Especially in recent years, the rights of transgender individuals have come to the forefront, highlighting both the milestones achieved and the challenges that persist. Whether it's debates about access to healthcare, recognition on official documents, or the right to serve in military roles, trans rights have become emblematic of the present-day challenges faced by the LGBTQ+ community.

It's essential to recognize that while we have come a long way, the path forward may still be fraught with obstacles. The events of the past serve not just as a record of what has been accomplished, but also as a beacon for what still needs to be done. The timeline underscores the importance of continued advocacy, solidarity, and vigilance in ensuring that the rights of all members of the LGBTQ+ community are recognized and protected, today and in the future.

Epilogue

A Letter from the Author

Dear Reader,

As I pen down this letter, I'm swept away by a wave of memories. Memories of my high school years, of the fear and anticipation, the knot in my stomach and the immense relief when I finally came out.

New York has been home since I was 5 years old, a far cry from my birthplace in Ukraine. I was embraced by loving arms, my adopted parents, who provided me with the warmth of a family, and the Big Apple taught me resilience and hustle. My father, however, was a chapter in my life that ended all too soon, passing away when I was just 7. Although he never knew about this part of my identity, I like to believe his love was unconditional, a love that would've encompassed me just the same.

Being open and proud of who I am was a journey. I've been blessed with incredible support, but I understand that my story, though filled with its own set of challenges, was a fortunate one in this respect. Not every coming out story receives applause, acceptance, or even understanding. Some tales are marred by tears, rejections, or silence. But every single one is significant, unique, and powerful in its own right.

To you, reading this, I want to say: Whether your story is sung from rooftops or whispered in quiet corners, it matters. You matter. To those who've known you for ages and to those you haven't met yet, you bring a world of difference. The universe has a way of sending us signs, people, and moments that tell us we're not alone.

Keep being you, unapologetically and bravely. You are a beacon of hope, love, and authenticity. Your journey, no matter how challenging, adds to the rich tapestry of life and brings light to the world. Remember always that you matter, and you are irreplaceably important to the world.

With love and pride,
Liam Sawyer

A Letter from the Author

Dear Reader,

About the Author

Liam Sawyer, born on February 5th in the picturesque landscapes
 of Ukraine, embarked on a transformative journey at the tender age of five. Alongside his sister, Caitlyn, he was adopted into a world of boundless love and opportunities. Today, he calls Staten Island, NY, his home, where he cherishes every moment with his mother, June, and his loyal canine companion, Deacon.

With a natural inclination towards technology, Liam pursued his passion and graduated with a Bachelor's degree in Computer Engineering. He now navigates the bustling streets of New York City as an IT Engineer, leaving an indelible mark in the tech world.

Other Books Written By Liam Sawyer

Wishes Of Love: A Memoir Of Love, Hope, And Family
Published 2020

Join Liam Sawyer on an extraordinary journey from Europe to the heart of America, where a young boy's longing for love becomes the driving force behind his poignant story. In "Wishes of Love," Liam shares his deeply personal adoption journey, reminding us that family is defined by the bonds of the heart, not by blood.

Whispers Of Hope: Poetic Reflections On Family And Life
Published 2023

"Whispers of Hope: Poetic Reflections on Family and Life" is a powerful collection of quotes by Liam Sawyer, each one reflecting the author's unique journey from his humble beginnings in Ukraine to the bustling life of New York City.